T0206799

THE Panda
CUB SWAP

Beth Bacon

THE Panda CUB SWAP

Illustrated by Anne Belov

Histria Kids

Las Vegas • Chicago • Palm Beach

**Published in the United States of America by
Histria Books, a division of Histria LLC
7181 N. Hualapai Way, Ste. 130-86
Las Vegas, NV 89166 USA
HistriaBooks.com**

Histria Kids is an imprint of Histria Books. Titles published under the imprints of Histria Books are distributed worldwide.

**Library of Congress Control Number: 2022936003
ISBN 978-1-59211-164-0 (hardcover)
ISBN 978-1-59211-249-4 (Ebook)**

In memory of Mark Karlins.
B. B.

To the memory of Ruth Belov Gross; my favorite cousin
and writer of picture books, including one about pandas.
A. B.

Lun Lun the giant panda was restless. She moved around her den more than usual, pacing and dragging straw into a pile.

In the workroom nearby, Rebecca and Deng looked into the Panda Cam. They smiled.

"She's building up her nest," said Rebecca.

"Motherhood comes naturally to Lun Lun," added Deng.

A newborn cub was on its way.

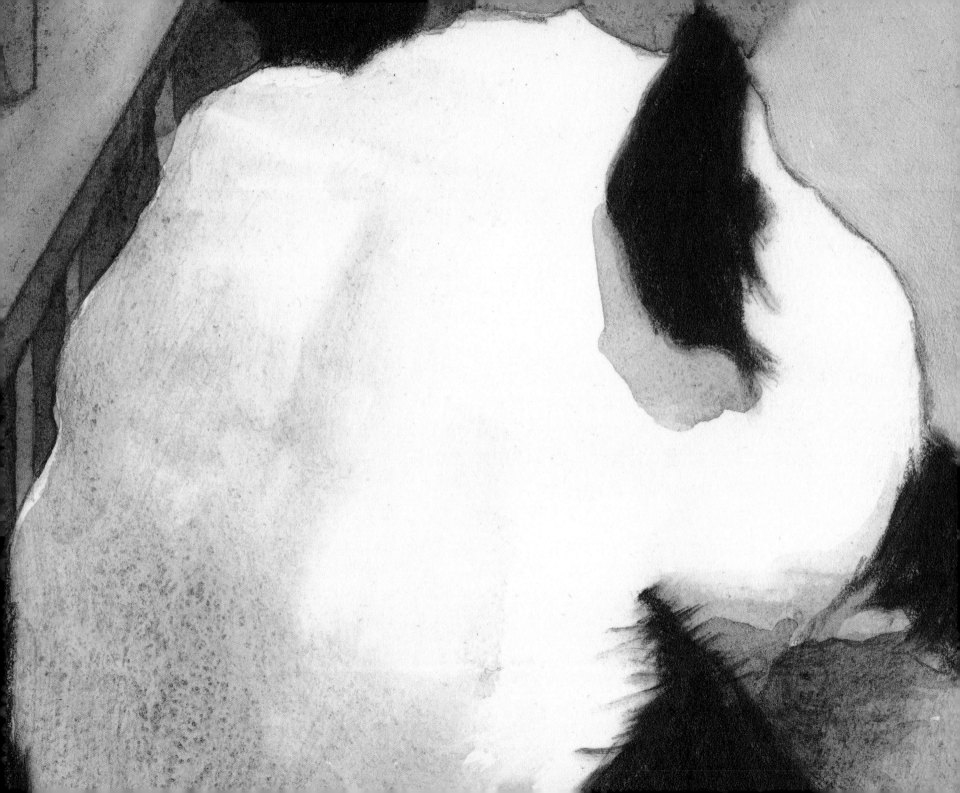

A little while later, a tiny, pink cub appeared on the Panda Cam. Rebecca, Deng, and the other zookeepers cheered. Then they gasped. A second tiny, pink cub surprised them all. Two cubs were always a possibility, but until this moment, no one knew for sure that Lun Lun was having twins. Two brand new, squirming, wiggling cubs made the team at Zoo Atlanta very happy. It also made them very nervous.

They were nervous because caring for newborn pandas takes a lot of work—so much work that panda mamas cannot take care of both cubs at once.

Panda cubs are born without fur. So they need their mama's hugs to keep warm.

Their eyes stay shut for almost two months, so they need their mama to see for them.

Their legs cannot support them yet, so their mama must carry them everywhere.

Panda cubs can't even go to the bathroom without help!

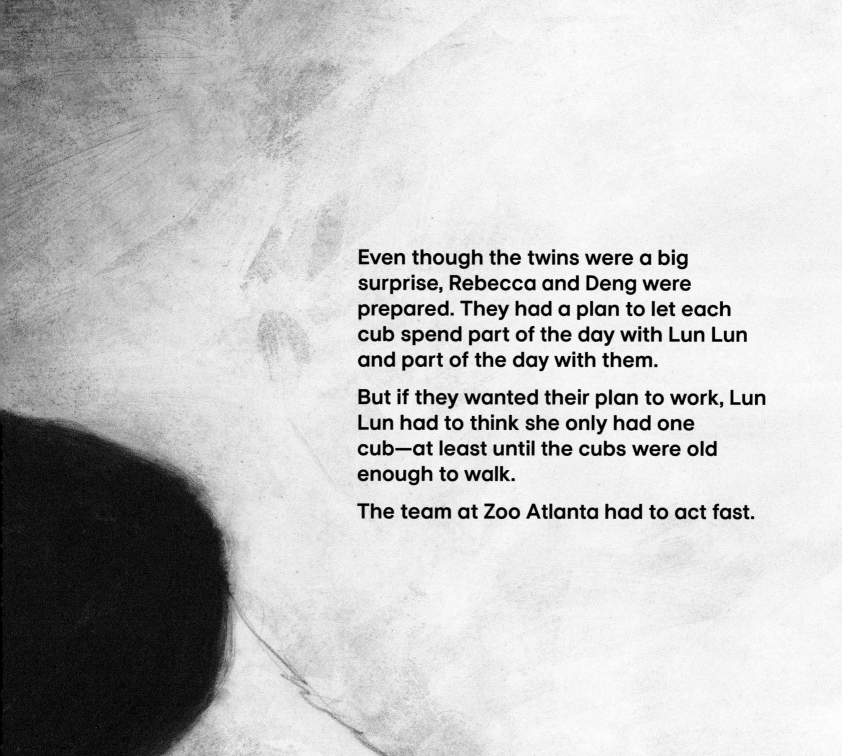

Even though the twins were a big surprise, Rebecca and Deng were prepared. They had a plan to let each cub spend part of the day with Lun Lun and part of the day with them.

But if they wanted their plan to work, Lun Lun had to think she only had one cub—at least until the cubs were old enough to walk.

The team at Zoo Atlanta had to act fast.

While Lun Lun huddled with the first cub, a keeper snuck into the den and quickly whisked away the other.

The team would take good care of the cubs in the workroom. But the zoo workroom was not as cozy as Lun Lun's embrace. If the cub swap worked, the cubs would take turns snuggling in Lun Lun's fur, listening to her heartbeat, and basking in her warmth.

The team at Zoo Atlanta liked the plan. But would Lun Lun like it too?

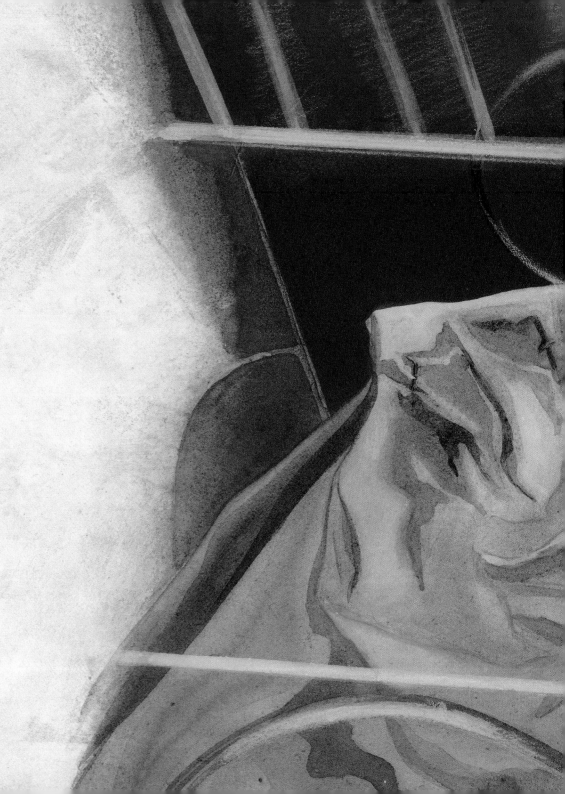

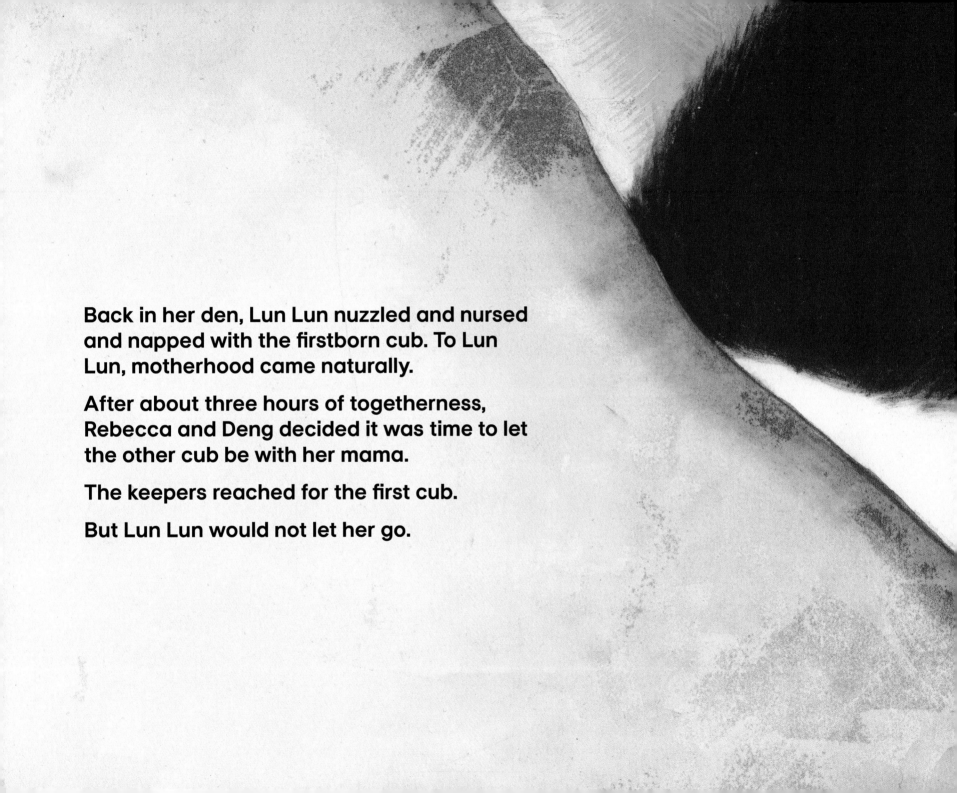

Back in her den, Lun Lun nuzzled and nursed and napped with the firstborn cub. To Lun Lun, motherhood came naturally.

After about three hours of togetherness, Rebecca and Deng decided it was time to let the other cub be with her mama.

The keepers reached for the first cub.

But Lun Lun would not let her go.

The panda cub swap was not off to a good start.

Then Deng had an idea.

"Lun Lun must be hungry," he said. "Let's put something tasty at the far end of her den. Maybe she will put down the cub and come get some food."

Rebecca stood across the den with some sweet sugar cane stalks. Lun Lun held tight to the cub.

Rebecca shook the stalks. Maybe the movement would capture Lun Lun's attention.

But instead of looking up, Lun Lun lowered her chin and snuggled the cub even closer.

Next, Rebecca tapped the stalks together. Clack, clack, clack! The sugar canes made a short, sharp sound.

Lun Lun lifted her head. She saw the treat. She gently placed the cub in her nest box and moved slowly toward the food.

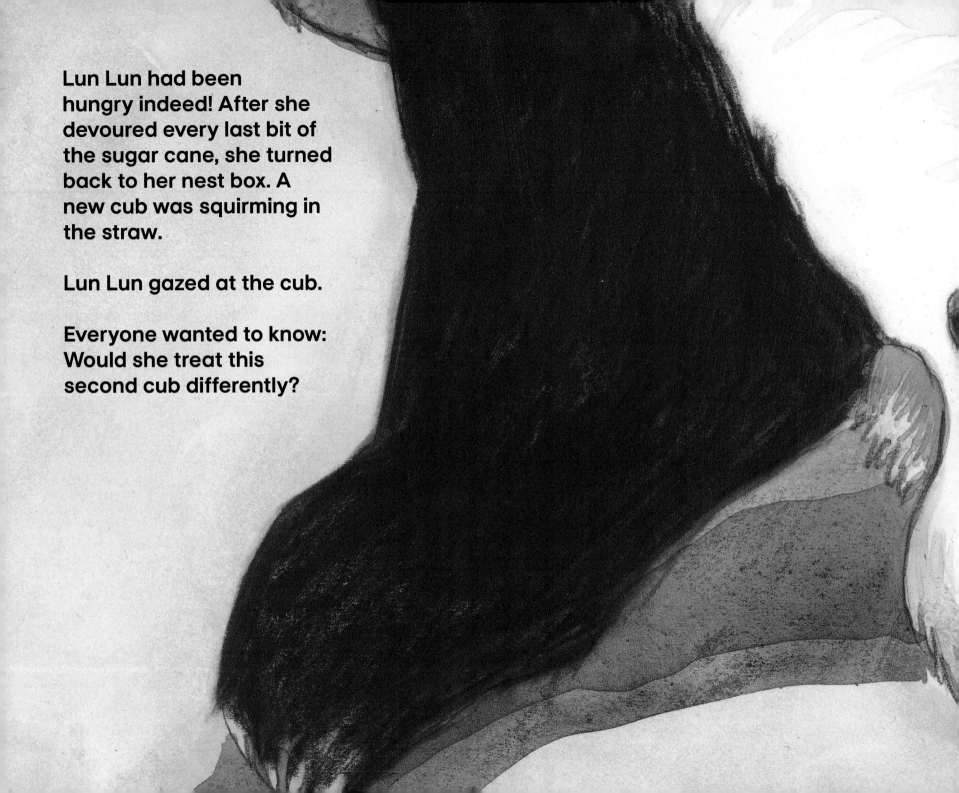

Lun Lun had been hungry indeed! After she devoured every last bit of the sugar cane, she turned back to her nest box. A new cub was squirming in the straw.

Lun Lun gazed at the cub.

Everyone wanted to know: Would she treat this second cub differently?

Rebecca and Deng held their breath.

Lun Lun lowered her head. She scanned the new cub from nose to tail.

Finally, in one gentle motion, Lun Lun picked up the cub and held her tight. To Lun Lun, motherhood came naturally.

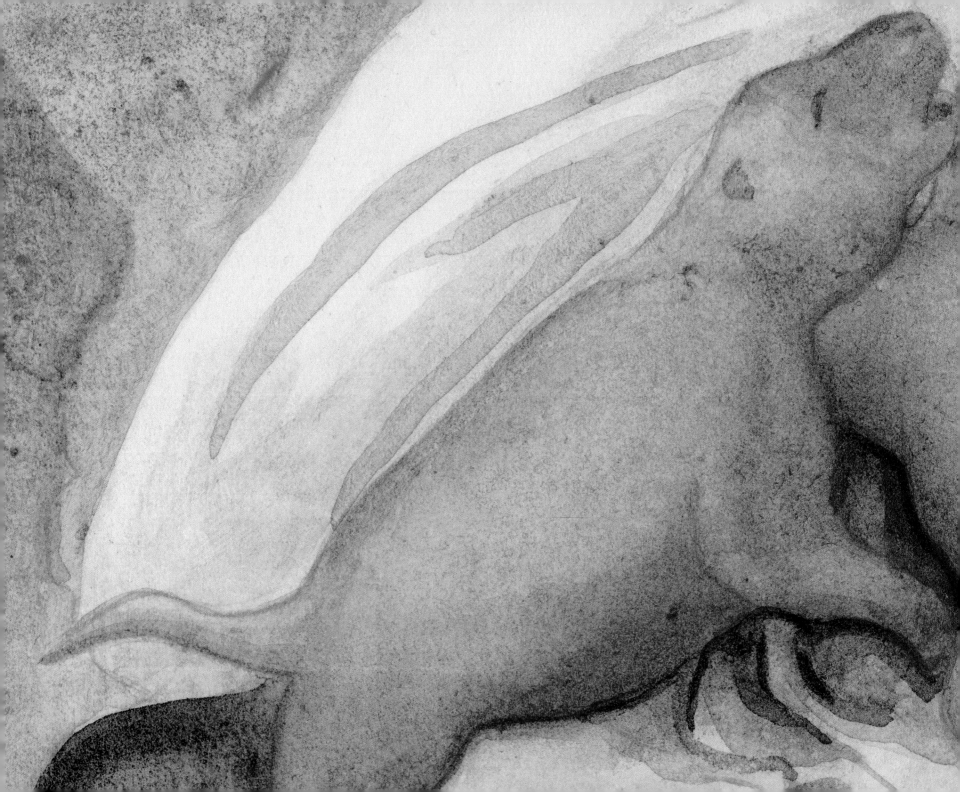

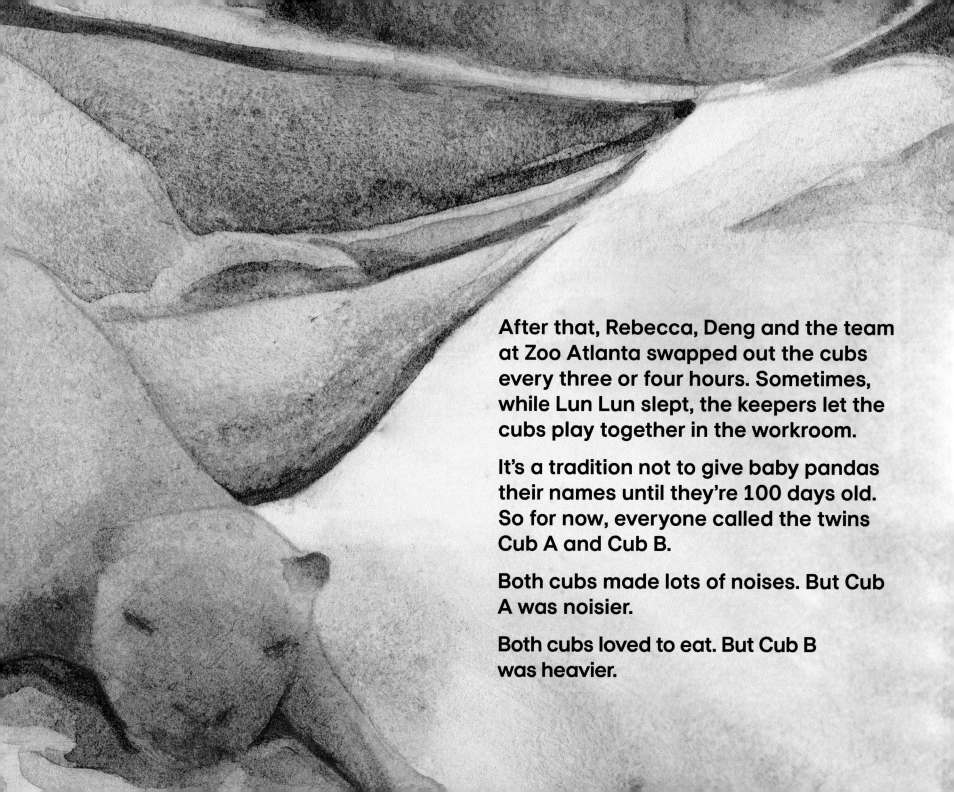

After that, Rebecca, Deng and the team at Zoo Atlanta swapped out the cubs every three or four hours. Sometimes, while Lun Lun slept, the keepers let the cubs play together in the workroom.

It's a tradition not to give baby pandas their names until they're 100 days old. So for now, everyone called the twins Cub A and Cub B.

Both cubs made lots of noises. But Cub A was noisier.

Both cubs loved to eat. But Cub B was heavier.

Taking care of panda cubs was
an around-the-clock job for both
Lun Lun and the keepers. At night,
after all the visitors left the zoo,
the workroom stayed busy.

It would be many months before the cubs were strong enough to walk. Only then could the keepers bring Mama and the babies together. For now, the keepers carried the cubs wherever they needed to go.

Week by week, the cubs grew bigger.

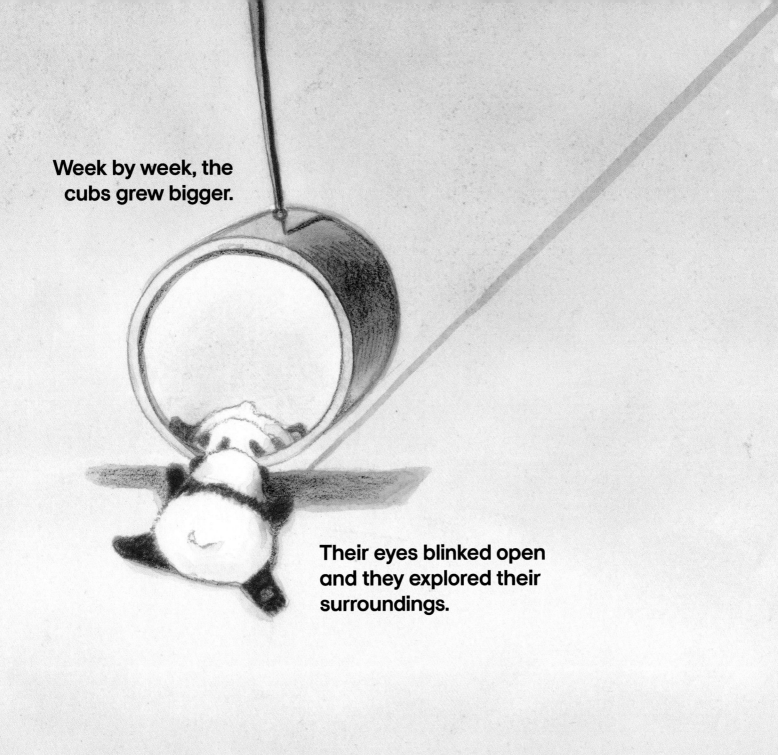

Their eyes blinked open and they explored their surroundings.

Black and white fur filled in over their pink skin.

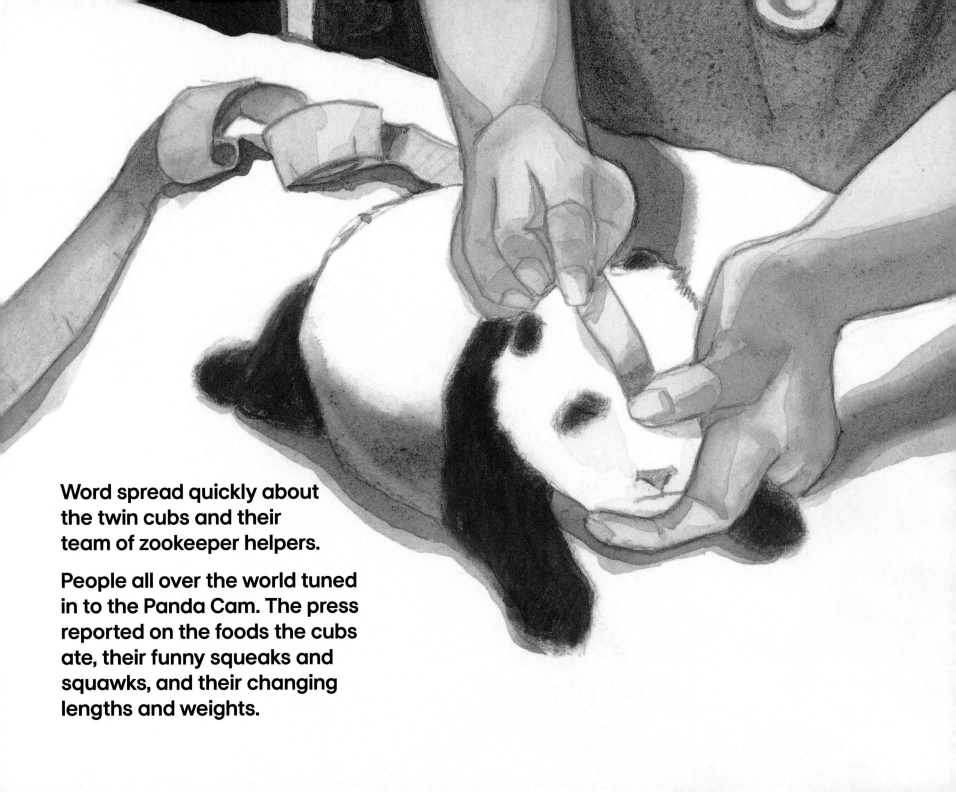

Word spread quickly about the twin cubs and their team of zookeeper helpers.

People all over the world tuned in to the Panda Cam. The press reported on the foods the cubs ate, their funny squeaks and squawks, and their changing lengths and weights.

Everyone seemed to know
about the panda swap.
Everyone except Lun Lun.

One hundred days after they were born, Cub A and Cub B got new names: Mei Lun and Mei Huan. In Chinese, the saying "mei lun mei huan" means "something indescribably beautiful and magnificent."

On naming day, the cubs twisted, squirmed, and reached. They were big enough to bounce and roll and play, but they were not yet big enough to walk.

Learning to walk is hard
work for baby pandas.

Very slowly, Mei Lun and
Mei Huan would stand up,
reach a paw forward and then...

SPLAT! PLOP!
They would fall
on their bellies.

They would tumble and roll.

Little by little, they would scoot across the floor. They were curious. And determined.

Then one day, Mei Huan climbed out of her nest box. Soon after, Mei Lun crawled out, too. The cubs were finally strong enough to walk. The time had come to bring them together with their mama.

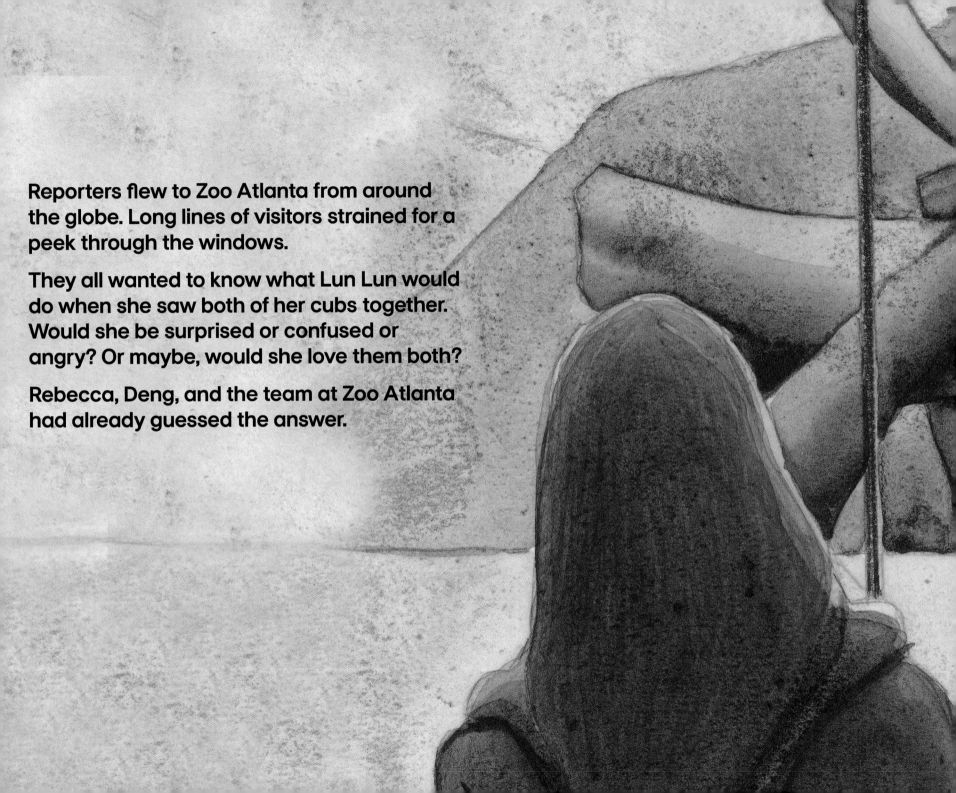

Reporters flew to Zoo Atlanta from around the globe. Long lines of visitors strained for a peek through the windows.

They all wanted to know what Lun Lun would do when she saw both of her cubs together. Would she be surprised or confused or angry? Or maybe, would she love them both?

Rebecca, Deng, and the team at Zoo Atlanta had already guessed the answer.

To Lun Lun, motherhood
came naturally.

NOTES ABOUT PANDAS

This is the story of Lun Lun and two of her cubs, Mei Lun and Mei Huan. But these two cubs are not Lun Lun's only offspring. Lun Lun has been an excellent mother to them all.

LUN LUN'S OTHER CUBS

Lun Lun has given birth to seven cubs. Mei Lan, a male, was born in 2006. Xi Lan, a male, was born in 2008. Po, a female, was born in 2010, followed by the twins in this story, Mei Lun and Mei Huan. Then in 2016, twins Ya Lun and Xi Lun were born.

Today Lun Lun is even a grandmother! Her first three cubs, Mei Lan, Xi Lan, and Po, now all have cubs of their own. All of Lun Lun's cubs, except Ya Lun and Xi Lun, are currently in China. Zoo Atlanta made an agreement to return Lun Lun's cubs to the Chengdu Research Base when they were big enough.

PAPA BEAR

You may wonder about the papa bear, Yang Yang. He also lives at Zoo Atlanta, but does not have a role in this story. Pandas do not live in family units. In the wild, they are solitary animals outside of mating season.

Lun Lun and Yang Yang were both born in 1997 at the Chengdu Base and were playmates starting from the time they were both about one year old. They traveled to Zoo Atlanta in November, 1999. Today they are well loved by visitors in Atlanta—and by Panda Cam watchers around the world.

THE PANDA SWAP

Panda cubs usually weigh only four ounces or less at birth. They are extremely vulnerable. The twin-swapping method in this story was developed at the Wolong and Chengdu Panda Bases around 2005. Mei Lun and Mei Huan's birth was the first panda swap to succeed outside of China. This practice has helped the captive panda population rise from around 200 to the current levels of roughly 600.

Lun Lun and her keepers at Zoo Atlanta have developed exceptional trust over the years. Like most animals, pandas have a strong instinct to protect their young. Without the trust between Lun Lun and her care staff, the swapping might not have been successful.

LUN LUN'S DIET

In this story, the keepers use sugar cane to tempt Lun Lun to eat. Giant pandas love sugar cane as a treat. But they have evolved primarily to eat bamboo. They will also eat meat if they have the chance.

PANDAS IN THE WILD

Giant pandas in the wild can only be found in China. Experts believe about 1,800 pandas live in the wild. A main reason for this low number is the deforestation of the mountainous regions of China where they live. Dwindling forests can isolate groups of pandas and can prevent the species from thriving. China has proposed establishing a 10,476-square mile park to create a "panda corridor." This will allow pandas to roam more and create a more sustainable wild population. Pandas are considered an "umbrella species." This means that when panda habitat is protected, other species living in the same area are protected, too.

PANDAS IN CAPTIVITY

Roughly 600 giant pandas live in captivity. Zoos around the world work very closely with research facilities in China to increase the panda population. Pandas used to be considered endangered, but their status has been changed to vulnerable. Some giant pandas born in captivity have had the chance to be introduced back into the wild. Pandas born in zoos such as Zoo Atlanta have too much human contact to be introduced to the wild.

For more information

If you want to learn more about giant pandas, please visit the websites of Zoo Atlanta, the Smithsonian National Zoo, and the Memphis Zoo. Pandas International and PDXWildlife are other good sources for information on pandas.

Notes and resources compiled by Anne Belov and Patricia Rice. Special thanks to Zoo Atlanta.

Beth Bacon

Beth Bacon is an author for young readers. Her books, *I Hate Reading* and *The Book No One Wants To Read* bring humor to the experiences of struggling readers. Her books *Covid-19 Helpers* and *Helping Our World Get Well: Covid Vaccines* offer children a clear understanding of the global pandemic. Beth volunteers for Open Hearts Big Dreams, an organization dedicated to improving literacy in Ethiopia. Beth has an MFA in Writing for Children and Young Adults from Vermont College of Fine Arts. She also has a MA in Media Ecology from New York University and a BA in Literature from Harvard University. Check out her work at www.BethBaconAuthor.com.

Anne Belov

Illustrator Anne Belov lives on an island in the Puget Sound, surrounded by tall trees and the occasional grove of bamboo. Her love of pandas came early in life, via stuffed pandas and books about them. When Mei Lun and Mei Huan were born, she danced around the kitchen in excitement while screaming into the phone to another lover of pandas who was also watching the birth on the Panda Cam. Anne has traveled to see pandas in five countries, including China, where she saw more pandas than she could count.

For these and other great books
for children and young adults visit
HistriaBooks.com

THE Panda
CUB SWAP